THE PANTHER AND THE LASH

BOOKS BY *Langston Hughes*

POETRY
THE PANTHER AND THE LASH (1967)
ASK YOUR MAMA (1961)
SELECTED POEMS OF LANGSTON HUGHES (1958)
MONTAGE OF A DREAM DEFERRED (1951)
ONE-WAY TICKET (1949)
FIELDS OF WONDER (1947)
SHAKESPEARE IN HARLEM (1942)
THE DREAM-KEEPER (1932)
FINE CLOTHES TO THE JEW (1927)
THE WEARY BLUES (1926)

FICTION
FIVE PLAYS BY LANGSTON HUGHES (1963)
SOMETHING IN COMMON AND OTHER STORIES (1963)
THE SWEET FLYPAPER OF LIFE (1955)
LAUGHING TO KEEP FROM CRYING (1952)
THE WAYS OF WHITE FOLKS (1934)
NOT WITHOUT LAUGHTER (1930)

HUMOR
SIMPLE'S UNCLE SAM (1965)
BEST OF SIMPLE (1961)
SIMPLE STAKES A CLAIM (1957)
SIMPLE TAKES A WIFE (1953)
SIMPLE SPEAKS HIS MIND (1950)

FOR YOUNG PEOPLE
FIRST BOOK OF AFRICA (1964)
THE FIRST BOOK OF THE WEST INDIES (1956)
THE FIRST BOOK OF RHYTHMS (1954)
THE FIRST BOOK OF JAZZ (1954)
THE FIRST BOOK OF THE NEGROES (1952)
—with Arna Bontemps
POPO AND FIFINA (1932)

BIOGRAPHY AND AUTOBIOGRAPHY
FAMOUS NEGRO HEROES OF AMERICA (1958)
I WONDER AS I WANDER (1956)
FAMOUS NEGRO MUSIC-MAKERS (1955)
FAMOUS AMERICAN NEGROES (1954)
THE BIG SEA (1940)

ANTHOLOGY
THE LANGSTON HUGHES READER (1958)

HISTORY
—with Milton Meltzer
BLACK MAGIC: A PICTORIAL HISTORY OF THE NEGRO IN AMERICAN
    ENTERTAINMENT (1967)
FIGHT FOR FREEDOM: THE STORY OF THE NAACP (1962)
—with Milton Meltzer
A PICTORIAL HISTORY OF THE NEGRO IN AMERICA (1956)

LANGSTON HUGHES

Vintage Classics

VINTAGE BOOKS
A DIVISION OF RANDOM HOUSE, INC.
NEW YORK

THE PANTHER & THE LASH

POEMS OF OUR TIMES

First Vintage Classics Edition, February 1992

Certain poems in this collection were previously published in the following books by
Langston Hughes:

Ask Your Mama (1961): "Cultural Exchange"
Fields of Wonder (1947): "Words Like Freedom," "Oppression," "Dream Dust"
The Langston Hughes Reader (1958): "Elderly Leaders" under the title "Elderly Politicians"
Montage of a Dream Deferred (1951): "Corner Meeting," "Motto," "Children's Rhymes"
One-Way Ticket (1949): "Harlem" under the title "Puzzled," "Who But the Lord?," "Third
   Degree," "October 16: The Raid," "Still Here," "Florida Road Workers," "Freedom" under the
   title "Democracy," "Warning" under the title "Roland Hayes Beaten," "Daybreak in
   Alabama"
Scottsboro Limited (1932): "Christ in Alabama," "Justice"
Selected Poems of Langston Hughes (1959): "Dream Deferred" under the title "Harlem,"
   "American Heartbreak," "Georgia Dusk," "Jim Crow Car" under the title "Lunch in a Jim
   Crow Car"
Shakespeare in Harlem (1942): "Ku Klux," "Merry-Go-Round"

Library of Congress Cataloging-in-Publication Data
Hughes, Langston, 1902–1967.
      The panther & the lash : poems of our times / Langston Hughes. —
   1st Vintage classics ed.
         p.   cm. — (Vintage classics)
      ISBN 0-679-73659-X
      1. Afro-Americans—Poetry.   I. Title.   II. Title: Panther and the
   lash.   III. Series.
   PS3515.U274P3   1992
   811'.52—dc20   91-50087
                              CIP

Manufactured in the United States of America
B987654

The author wishes to thank the editors of the following publications which first printed the poems specified:

American Dialog: "Final Call" (1964)
Black Orpheus: "Angola Question Mark" (1959)
Colorado Review: "Where? When? Which?" (Winter 1956–7)
Crisis: "Question and Answer" (1966)
Free Lance: "Without Benefit of Declaration" (1955)
Harper's Magazine: "Long View: Negro" (1965)
Liberator: "Junior Addict" (1963), "Frederick Douglass" (1966),
      "Northern Liberal" (1963)
The Nation: "Crowns and Garlands" (1967)
Negro Digest: "Mississippi" (1965), "Dinner Guest: Me" (1965)
Opportunity: "History" (1934)
Phylon: "Little Song on Housing" (1955), "Vari-Colored Song" (1952)
La Poesie Negro-Americaine (1966): "Bible Belt" under the title
      "Not for Publication—Defense de Publier"
Voices: "Down Where I Am" (1950)

To Rosa Parks of Montgomery

who started it all when, on
being ordered to get up and
stand at the back of the bus
where there were no seats left,
she said simply, "My feet are
tired," and did not move, thus
setting off in 1955 the boy-
cotts, the sit-ins, the Free-
dom Rides, the petitions, the
marches, the voter registration
drives, and *I Shall Not Be
Moved.*

Contents

WORDS ON FIRE

CORNER MEETING

Ladder, flag, and amplifier
now are what the soap box
used to be.

The speaker catches fire,
looking at listeners' faces.

His words jump down
to stand
in their
places.

HARLEM

Here on the edge of hell
Stands Harlem—
Remembering the old lies,
The old kicks in the back,
The old "Be patient"
They told us before.

Sure, we remember.
Now when the man at the corner store
Says sugar's gone up another two cents,
And bread one,
And there's a new tax on cigarettes—
We remember the job we never had,
Never could get,
And can't have now
Because we're colored.

So we stand here
On the edge of hell
In Harlem
And look out on the world
And wonder
What we're gonna do
In the face of what
We remember.

PRIME

Uptown on Lenox Avenue
Where a nickel costs a dime,
In these lush and thieving days
When million-dollar thieves
Glorify their million-dollar ways
In the press and on the radio and TV—
　　But won't let me
　　Skim even a dime—
I, black, come to my prime
In the section of the niggers
Where a nickel costs a dime.

CROWNS AND GARLANDS

Make a garland of Leontynes and Lenas
And hang it about your neck
    Like a lei.
Make a crown of Sammys, Sidneys, Harrys,
Plus Cassius Mohammed Ali Clay.
Put their laurels on your brow
    Today—
Then before you can walk
To the neighborhood corner,
Watch them droop, wilt, fade
    Away.
Though worn in glory on my head,
They do not last a day—
    Not one—
Nor take the place of meat or bread
Or rent that I must pay.
Great names for crowns and garlands!
    Yeah!
I love Ralph Bunche—
But I can't eat him for lunch.

ELDERLY LEADERS

The old, the cautious, the over-wise—
Wisdom reduced to the personal equation:
Life is a system of half-truths and lies,
Opportunistic, convenient evasion.
    Elderly,
    Famous,
    Very well paid,
    They clutch at the egg
    Their master's
    Goose laid:
    $$$$$
    $$$$
    $$$
    $$
    $
    .

THE BACKLASH BLUES

Mister Backlash, Mister Backlash,
Just who do you think I am?
Tell me, Mister Backlash,
Who do you think I am?
You raise my taxes, freeze my wages,
Send my son to Vietnam.

You give me second-class houses,
Give me second-class schools,
Second-class houses
And second-class schools.
You must think us colored folks
Are second-class fools.

When I try to find a job
To earn a little cash,
Try to find myself a job
To earn a little cash,
All you got to offer
Is a white backlash.

But the world is big,
The world is big and round,
Great big world, Mister Backlash,
Big and bright and round—
And it's full of folks like me who are
Black, Yellow, Beige, and Brown.

Mister Backlash, Mister Backlash,
What do you think I got to lose?
Tell me, Mister Backlash,
What you think I got to lose?
I'm gonna leave you, Mister Backlash,
Singing your mean old backlash blues.

> *You're the one,*
> *Yes, you're the one*
> *Will have the blues.*

LENOX AVENUE BAR

Weaving
between assorted terrors
is the Jew
who owns the place—
one Jew,
fifty Negroes:
embroideries
(heirloomed
from ancient evenings)
tattered
in this neon
place.

MOTTO

I play it cool
And dig all jive—
That's the reason
I stay alive.

My motto,
As I live and learn
      Is
Dig and be dug
In return.

JUNIOR ADDICT

The little boy
who sticks a needle in his arm
and seeks an out in other worldly dreams,
who seeks an out in eyes that droop
and ears that close to Harlem screams,
cannot know, of course,
(and has no way to understand)
a sunrise that he cannot see
beginning in some other land—
but destined sure to flood—and soon—
the very room in which he leaves
his needle and his spoon,
the very room in which today the air
is heavy with the drug
of his despair.

    (Yet little can
    tomorrow's sunshine give
    to one who will not live.)

Quick, sunrise, come—
Before the mushroom bomb
Pollutes his stinking air
With better death

Than is his living here,
With viler drugs
Than bring today's release
In poison from the fallout
Of our peace.

> *"It's easier to get dope
> than it is to get a job."*

Yes, easier to get dope
than to get a job—
daytime or nightime job,
teen-age, pre-draft,
pre-lifetime job.

Quick, sunrise, come!
Sunrise out of Africa,
Quick, come!
Sunrise, please come!
Come! Come!

DREAM DEFERRED

What happens to a dream deferred?

Does it dry up
like a raisin in the sun?
Or fester like a sore—
And then run?
Does it stink like rotten meat?
Or crust and sugar over—
like a syrupy sweet?

Maybe it just sags
like a heavy load.

Or does it explode?

DEATH IN YORKVILLE

(James Powell, Summer, 1964)

How many bullets does it take
To kill a fifteen-year-old kid?
How many bullets does it take
To kill me?

How many centuries does it take
To bind my mind—chain my feet—
Rope my neck—lynch me—
Unfree?

From the slave chain to the lynch rope
To the bullets of Yorkville,
Jamestown, 1619 to 1963:
Emancipation Centennial—
100 years NOT free.

Civil War Centennial: 1965.
How many Centennials does it take
To kill me,
Still alive?

When the long hot summers come
Death ain't
No jive.

WHO BUT THE LORD?

I looked and I saw
That man they call the Law.
He was coming
Down the street at me!
I had visions in my head
Of being laid out cold and dead,
Or else murdered
By the third degree.

I said, O, Lord, if you can,
Save me from that man!
Don't let him make a pulp out of me!
But the Lord he was not quick.
The Law raised up his stick
And beat the living hell
Out of me!

Now I do not understand
Why God don't protect a man
From police brutality.
Being poor and black,
I've no weapon to strike back
So who but the Lord
Can protect me?

We'll see.

THIRD DEGREE

Hit me! Jab me!
Make me say I did it.
Blood on my sport shirt
And my tan suede shoes.

Faces like jack-o'-lanterns
In gray slouch hats.

Slug me! Beat me!
Scream jumps out
Like blowtorch.
Three kicks between the legs
That kill the kids
I'd make tomorrow.

Bars and floor skyrocket
And burst like Roman candles.

When you throw
Cold water on me,
I'll sign the
Paper . . .

BLACK PANTHER

Pushed into the corner
Of the hobnailed boot,
Pushed into the corner of the
"I-don't-want-to-die" cry,
Pushed into the corner of
"I don't want to study war no more,"
Changed into "Eye for eye,"
The Panther in his desperate boldness
Wears no disguise,
Motivated by the truest
Of the oldest
Lies.

FINAL CALL

SEND FOR THE PIED PIPER AND LET HIM PIPE THE RATS
  AWAY.
SEND FOR ROBIN HOOD TO CLINCH THE ANTI-POVERTY
  CAMPAIGN.
SEND FOR THE FAIRY QUEEN WITH A WAVE OF THE
  WAND
TO MAKE US ALL INTO PRINCES AND PRINCESSES.
SEND FOR KING ARTHUR TO BRING THE HOLY GRAIL.
SEND FOR OLD MAN MOSES TO LAY DOWN THE LAW.
SEND FOR JESUS TO PREACH THE SERMON ON THE
  MOUNT.
SEND FOR DREYFUS TO CRY, *J'ACCUSE!*
SEND FOR DEAD BLIND LEMON TO SING THE *B FLAT
  BLUES.*
SEND FOR ROBESPIERRE TO SCREAM, "*ÇA IRA! ÇA IRA!
  ÇA IRA!*"
SEND (GOD FORBID—HE'S NOT DEAD LONG ENOUGH!)
FOR LUMUMBA TO CRY "FREEDOM NOW!"
SEND FOR LAFAYETTE AND TELL HIM, "HELP! HELP ME!"

SEND FOR DENMARK VESEY CRYING, "FREE!"

FOR CINQUE SAYING, "RUN A NEW FLAG UP THE MAST."

FOR OLD JOHN BROWN WHO KNEW SLAVERY COULDN'T
      LAST.

SEND FOR LENIN! (DON'T YOU DARE!—HE CAN'T COME
      HERE!)

SEND FOR TROTSKY! (WHAT? DON'T CONFUSE THE ISSUE,
      PLEASE!)

SEND FOR UNCLE TOM ON HIS MIGHTY KNEES.

SEND FOR LINCOLN, SEND FOR GRANT.

SEND FOR FREDERICK DOUGLASS, GARRISON, BEECHER,
      LOWELL.

SEND FOR HARRIETT TUBMAN, OLD SOJOURNER TRUTH.

SEND FOR MARCUS GARVEY (WHAT?) SUFI (WHO?)
      FATHER DIVINE (WHERE?)

DuBOIS (WHEN?) MALCOLM (OH!) SEND FOR STOKELY.
      (NO?) THEN

SEND FOR ADAM POWELL ON A NON-SUBPOENA DAY.

SEND FOR THE PIED PIPER TO PIPE OUR RATS AWAY.

    (And if nobody comes, send for me.)

2

AMERICAN
HEARTBREAK

AMERICAN HEARTBREAK

I am the American heartbreak—
The rock on which Freedom
Stumped its toe—
The great mistake
That Jamestown made
Long ago.

GHOSTS OF 1619

Ghosts of all too solid flesh,
Dark ghosts come back to haunt you now,
These dark ghosts to taunt you—
Yet ghosts so solid, ghosts so real
They may not only haunt you—
But rape, rob, steal,
Sit-in, stand-in, stall-in, vote-in
(Even vote for real in Alabam')
And in voting not give a damn
For the fact that white *was* right
Until last night.

Last night?
What happened then?
Flesh-and-blood ghosts
Became flesh-and-blood men?
Got tired of asking, *When?*
Although minority,
Suddenly became majority
(Metaphysically speaking)
In seeking authority?

How can one man be ten?
Or ten be a hundred and ten?
Or a thousand and ten?
Or a million and ten
Are but a thousand and ten
Or a hundred and ten
Or ten——or one——
Or none——
Being ghosts
Of then?

OCTOBER 16: THE RAID

Perhaps
You will remember
John Brown.

John Brown
Who took his gun,
Took twenty-one companions
White and black,
Went to shoot your way to freedom
Where two rivers meet
And the hills of the
South
Look slow at one another—
And died
For your sake.

Now that you are
Many years free,
And the echo of the Civil War
Has passed away,
And Brown himself
Has long been tried at law,
Hanged by the neck,
And buried in the ground—
Since Harpers Ferry
Is alive with ghosts today,
Immortal raiders
Come again to town—

Perhaps
You will recall
John Brown.

LONG VIEW: NEGRO

Emancipation: 1865
Sighted through the
Telescope of dreams
Looms larger,
So much larger,
So it seems,
Than truth can be.

But turn the telescope around,
Look through the larger end—
And wonder why
What was so large
Becomes so small
Again.

FREDERICK DOUGLASS: 1817–1895

Douglass was someone who,
Had he walked with wary foot
And frightened tread,
From very indecision
Might be dead,
Might have lost his soul,
But instead decided to be bold
And capture every street
On which he set his feet,
To route each path
Toward freedom's goal,
To make each highway
Choose *his* compass' choice,
To all the world cried,
Hear my voice! . . .
Oh, to be a beast, a bird,
Anything but a slave! he said.

Who would be free
Themselves must strike
The first blow, he said.

　　　He died in 1895.
　　　He is not dead.

STILL HERE

I been scared and battered.
My hopes the wind done scattered.
    Snow has friz me,
    Sun has baked me,
Looks like between 'em they done
    Tried to make me
Stop laughin', stop lovin', stop livin'—
    But I don't care!
    I'm still here!

WORDS LIKE FREEDOM

There are words like *Freedom*
Sweet and wonderful to say.
On my heartstrings freedom sings
All day everyday.

There are words like *Liberty*
That almost make me cry.
If you had known what I know
You would know why.

THE BIBLE BELT

CHRIST IN ALABAMA

Christ is a nigger,
Beaten and black:
Oh, bare your back!

Mary is His mother:
Mammy of the South,
Silence your mouth.

God is His father:
White Master above
Grant Him your love.

Most holy bastard
Of the bleeding mouth,
    Nigger Christ
    On the cross
    Of the South.

BIBLE BELT

It would be too bad if Jesus
Were to come back black.
There are so many churches
Where he could not pray
In the U.S.A.,
Where entrance to Negroes,
No matter how sanctified,
Is denied,
Where race, not religion,
Is glorified.
But say it—
You may be
Crucified.

MILITANT

Let all who will
Eat quietly the bread of shame.
I cannot,
Without complaining loud and long,
Tasting its bitterness in my throat,
And feeling to my very soul
It's wrong.
For honest work
You proffer me poor pay,
For honest dreams
Your spit is in my face,
And so my fist is clenched
Today—
To strike your face.

OFFICE BUILDING: EVENING

When the white folks get through
    Here come you:

    Got to clean awhile.

When daytime folks
Have made their dough,
    Away they go:

    You clean awhile.

When white collars get done,
    You have your "fun"
    Cleaning awhile.

"But just wait, chile . . ."

FLORIDA ROAD WORKERS

Hey, Buddy!
Look at me!

I'm makin' a road
For the cars to fly by on,
Makin' a road
Through the palmetto thicket
For light and civilization
To travel on.

I'm makin' a road
For the rich to sweep over
In their big cars
And leave me standin' here.

Sure,
A road helps everybody.
Rich folks ride—
And I get to see 'em ride.
I ain't never seen nobody
Ride so fine before.

Hey, Buddy, look!
I'm makin' a road!

SPECIAL BULLETIN

Lower the flags
For the dead become alive,
Play hillbilly dirges
That hooded serpents may dance,
Write obituaries
For white-robed warriors
Emerging to the fanfare
Of death rattles.
Muffled drums in Swanee River tempo.
Hand-high salutes—*heil!*
Present arms
With ax handles
Made in Atlanta,
    Sieg
    Heil!
Oh, run, all who have not
Changed your names.
As for you others—
The skin on your black face,
Peel off the skin,
    Peel peel
    Peel off
    The skin.

MISSISSIPPI

Oh, what sorrow!
Oh, what pity!
Oh, what pain
That tears and blood
Should mix like rain
And terror come again
To Mississippi.

Again?
Where has terror been?
On vacation? Up North?
In some other section
Of the Nation,
Lying low, unpublicized,
Masked—with only
Jaundiced eyes showing
Through the mask?

What sorrow, pity, pain,
That tears and blood
Still mix like rain
In Mississippi.

KU KLUX

They took me out
To some lonesome place.
They said, "Do you believe
In the great white race?"

I said, "Mister,
To tell you the truth,
I'd believe in anything
If you'd just turn me loose."

The white man said, "Boy,
Can it be
You're a-standin' there
A-sassin' me?"

They hit me in the head
And knocked me down.
And then they kicked me
On the ground.

A klansman said, "Nigger,
Look me in the face—
And tell me you believe in
The great white race."

JUSTICE

That Justice is a blind goddess
Is a thing to which we black are wise:
Her bandage hides two festering sores
That once perhaps were eyes.

BIRMINGHAM SUNDAY

(September 15, 1963)

Four little girls
Who went to Sunday School that day
And never came back home at all
But left instead
Their blood upon the wall
With spattered flesh
And bloodied Sunday dresses
Torn to shreds by dynamite
That China made aeons ago—
Did not know
That what China made
Before China was ever Red at all
Would redden with their blood
This Birmingham-on-Sunday wall.

Four tiny girls
Who left their blood upon that wall,
In little graves today await
The dynamite that might ignite
The fuse of centuries of Dragon Kings
Whose tomorrow sings a hymn
The missionaries never taught Chinese
In Christian Sunday School
To implement the Golden Rule.

      Four little girls
Might be awakened someday soon
By songs upon the breeze
As yet unfelt among magnolia trees.

BOMBINGS IN DIXIE

It's not enough to mourn
And not enough to pray.
Sackcloth and ashes, anyhow,
Save for another day.

The Lord God Himself
Would hardly desire
That men be burned to death—
And bless the fire.

CHILDREN'S RHYMES

By what sends
the white kids
I ain't sent:
I know I can't
be President.

What don't bug
them white kids
sure bugs me:
We know everybody
ain't free.

Lies written down
for white folks
ain't for us a-tall:
Liberty And Justice—
Huh!—For All?

DOWN WHERE I AM

Too many years
Beatin' at the door—
I done beat my
Both fists sore.

Too many years
Tryin' to get up there—
Done broke my ankles down,
Got nowhere.

Too many years
Climbin' that hill,
'Bout out of breath.
I got my fill.

I'm gonna plant my feet
On solid ground.
If you want to see me,
Come down.

4

THE FACE
OF WAR

MOTHER IN WARTIME

As if it were some noble thing,
She spoke of sons at war,
As if freedom's cause
Were pled anew at some heroic bar,
As if the weapons used today
Killed with great élan,
As if technicolor banners flew
To honor modern man—
Believing everything she read
In the daily news,
(No in-between to choose)
She thought that only
One side won,
Not that *both*
Might lose.

WITHOUT BENEFIT OF DECLARATION

Listen here, Joe,
Don't you know
That tomorrow
You got to go
Out yonder where
The steel winds blow?

Listen here, kid,
It's been said
Tomorrow you'll be dead
Out there where
The rain is lead.

Don't ask me why.
Just go ahead and die.
Hidden from the sky
Out yonder you'll lie:
A medal to your family—
In exchange for
    A guy.

Mama, don't cry.

OFFICIAL NOTICE

Dear Death:
I got your message
That my son is dead.
The ink you used
To write it
Is the blood he bled.
You say he died with honor
On the battlefield,
And that I am honored, too,
By this bloody yield.
Your letter
Signed in blood,
With his blood
Is sealed.

PEACE

We passed their graves:
The dead men there,
Winners or losers,
Did not care.

In the dark
They could not see
Who had gained
The victory.

LAST PRINCE OF THE EAST

Futile of me to offer you my hand,
Last little brown prince
Of Malaysia land.
Your wall is too high
And your moat is too wide—
For the white world's gunboats
Are all on your side.
So you lie in your cradle
And shake your rattle
To the jingo cry
Of blood and battle
While Revolt in the rice fields
Puts on a red gown.

Before you are king,
He'll come to town.

THE DOVE

. . . and here is
old Picasso and the dove
and dreams as fragile
as pottery with dove
in white on clay
dark brown as
earth is brown
from our old
battle ground . . .

WAR

The face of war is my face.
The face of war is your face.
    What color
    Is the face
    Of war?
Brown, black, white—
Your face and my face.

Death is the broom
I take in my hands
To sweep the world
    Clean.
I sweep and I sweep
Then mop and I mop.
I dip my broom in blood,
My mop in blood—
And blame you for this,
Because you are *there,*
    Enemy.

It's hard to blame me,
Because I am here—
So I kill you.
And you kill me.
        My name,
Like your name,
        Is war.

5

**AFRICAN
QUESTION MARK**

OPPRESSION

Now dreams
Are not available
To the dreamers,
Nor songs
To the singers.

In some lands
Dark night
And cold steel
Prevail—
But the dream
Will come back,
And the song
Break
Its jail.

ANGOLA QUESTION MARK

Don't know why I,
Black,
Must still stand
With my back
To the last frontier
Of fear
In my own land.

Don't know why I
Must turn into
A Mau Mau
And lift my hand
Against my fellow man
To live on my own land.

But it is so—
And being so
I know
For you and me
There's
Woe.

LUMUMBA'S GRAVE

Lumumba was black
And he didn't trust
The whores all powdered
With uranium dust.

Lumumba was black
And he didn't believe
The lies thieves shook
Through their "freedom" sieve.

Lumumba was black.
His blood was red—
And for being a man
They killed him dead.

They buried Lumumba
In an unmarked grave.
But he needs no marker—
For air is his grave.

Sun is his grave,
Moon is, stars are,
Space is his grave.

My heart's his grave,
And it's marked there.
Tomorrow will mark
It everywhere.

COLOR

Wear it
Like a banner
For the proud—
Not like a shroud.
Wear it
Like a song
Soaring high—
Not moan or cry.

QUESTION AND ANSWER

Durban, Birmingham,
Cape Town, Atlanta,
Johannesburg, Watts,
The earth around
Struggling, fighting,
Dying—for what?

A world to gain.

Groping, hoping,
Waiting—for what?

A world to gain.

Dreams kicked asunder,
Why not go under?

There's a world to gain.

But suppose I don't want it,
Why take it?

To remake it.

HISTORY

The past has been a mint
Of blood and sorrow.
That must not be
True of tomorrow.

6

DINNER GUEST: ME

DINNER GUEST: ME

I know I am
The Negro Problem
Being wined and dined,
Answering the usual questions
That come to white mind
Which seeks demurely
To probe in polite way
The why and wherewithal
Of darkness U.S.A.—
Wondering how things got this way
In current democratic night,
Murmuring gently
Over *fraises du bois,*
"I'm so ashamed of being white."

The lobster is delicious,
The wine divine,
And center of attention
At the damask table, mine.
To be a Problem on
Park Avenue at eight
Is not so bad.
Solutions to the Problem,
Of course, wait.

NORTHERN LIBERAL

And so
we lick our chops at Birmingham
and say, "See!
Southern dogs have vindicated me—
I knew that this would come."
But who are we to be
so proud that savages
have proven a point
taken late in time
to show how liberal I am?
Above the struggle
I can quite afford to be:
well-fed, degreed,
not beat—elite,
up North.
I send checks,
support your cause,
and lick my chops
at Jim Crow laws
and Birmingham—
where you,
not I
am.

SWEET WORDS ON RACE

Sweet words that take
Their own sweet time to flower
And then so quickly wilt
Within the inner ear,
Belie the budding promise
Of their pristine hour
To wither in the
Sultry air of fear.
Sweet words so brave
When danger is not near,
I've heard
So many times before,
I'd just as leave
Not hear them
Anymore.

UN-AMERICAN INVESTIGATORS

The committee's fat,
Smug, almost secure
Co-religionists
Shiver with delight
In warm manure
As those investigated—
Too brave to name a name—
Have pseudonyms revealed
In Gentile game
    Of who,
    Born Jew,
    Is who?
Is not your name Lipshitz?
    Yes.
Did you not change it
For subversive purposes?
    No.
For nefarious gain?
    Not so.
Are you sure?
The committee shivers
With delight in
Its manure.

SLAVE

To ride piggy-back
to the market of death
there to purchase a slave,
a slave who died young,
having given up breath—
unwittingly,
of course—
a slave who died young,
perhaps from a fix
with a rusty needle
infected,
to purchase a slave
to the market of death
I ride protected.

UNDERTOW

The solid citizens
Of the country club set,
Caught between
Selma and Peking,
Feel the rug of dividends,
Bathmats of pride,
Even soggy country club
Pink paper towels
Dropped on the MEN'S ROOM floor
Slipping out from under them
Like waves of sea
Between Selma, Peking,
Westchester
And me.

LITTLE SONG ON HOUSING

Here I come!
Been saving all my life
To get a nice home
For me and my wife.

> *White folks flee—*
> *As soon as you see*
> *My problems*
> *And me!*

Neighborhood's clean,
But the house is old,
Prices are doubled
When I get sold:
Still I buy.

> *White folks fly—*
> *Soon as you spy*
> *My wife*
> *And I!*

Next thing you know,
Our neighbors all colored are.
The candy store's
Turned into a bar:
White folks have left
The whole neighborhood
To my black self.

> *White folks, flee!*
> *Still—there is me!*
> *White folks, fly!*
> *Here am I!*

CULTURAL EXCHANGE

In the Quarter of the Negroes
Where the doors are doors of paper
Dust of dingy atoms
Blows a scratchy sound.
Amorphous jack-o'-lanterns caper
and the wind won't wait for midnight
For fun to blow doors down.

By the river and the railroad
With fluid far-off going
Boundaries bind unbinding
A whirl of whistles blowing.
No trains or steamboats going—
Yet Leontyne's unpacking.

In the Quarter of the Negroes
Where the doorknob lets in Lieder
More than German ever bore,
Her yesterday past grandpa—
Not of her own doing—
In a pot of collard greens
Is gently stewing.

Pushcarts fold and unfold
In a supermarket sea.
And we better find out, mama,
Where is the colored laundromat
Since we moved up to Mount Vernon.

In the pot behind the paper doors
On the old iron stove what's cooking?
What's smelling, Leontyne?
Lieder, lovely Lieder
And a leaf of collard green.
Lovely Lieder, Leontyne.

You know, right at Christmas
They asked me if my blackness,
Would it rub off?
I said, *Ask your mama.*

Dreams and nightmares!
Nightmares, dreams, oh!
Dreaming that the Negroes
Of the South have taken over—
Voted all the Dixiecrats
Right out of power—
Comes the COLORED HOUR:
Martin Luther King is Governor of Georgia,
Dr. Rufus Clement his Chief Adviser,

A. Philip Randolph the High Grand Worthy.
In white pillared mansions
Sitting on their wide verandas,
Wealthy Negroes have white servants,
White sharecroppers work the black plantations,
And colored children have white mammies:
> Mammy Faubus
> Mammy Eastland
> Mammy Wallace

Dear, dear darling old white mammies—
Sometimes even buried with our family.
> *Dear* old
> Mammy Faubus!

Culture, they say, *is a two-way street:*
Hand me my mint julep, mammy.
> Hurry up!
> Make haste!

FROSTING

Freedom
Is just frosting
On somebody else's
Cake—
And so must be
Till we
Learn how to
Bake.

IMPASSE

I could tell you,
If I wanted to,
What makes me
What I am.

But I don't
Really want to—
And you don't
Give a damn.

7

DAYBREAK
IN ALABAMA

FREEDOM

Freedom will not come
Today, this year
    Nor ever
Through compromise and fear.

I have as much right
As the other fellow has
    To stand
On my two feet
And own the land.

I tire so of hearing people say,
Let things take their course.
Tomorrow is another day.
I do not need my freedom when I'm dead.
I cannot live on tomorrow's bread.
    Freedom
    Is a strong seed
    Planted
    In a great need.
    I live here, too.
    I want freedom
    Just as you.

GO SLOW

Go *slow*, they say—
While the bite
Of the dog is fast.
Go *slow*, I hear—
While they tell me
You can't eat here!
You can't live here!
You can't work here!
Don't demonstrate! Wait!—
While they lock the gate.

Am I supposed to be God,
Or an angel with wings
And a halo on my head
While jobless I starve dead?
Am I supposed to forgive
And meekly live
Going slow, slow, slow,
Slow, slow, slow,
Slow, slow,
Slow,
Slow,
Slow?
????
???
??
?

MERRY-GO-ROUND

Colored child
at carnival

Where is the Jim Crow section
On this merry-go-round,
Mister, cause I want to ride?
Down South where I come from
White and colored
Can't sit side by side.
Down South on the train
There's a Jim Crow car.
On the bus we're put in the back—
But there ain't no back
To a merry-go-round!
Where's the horse
For a kid that's black?

DREAM DUST

Gather out of star-dust
    Earth-dust,
    Cloud-dust,
And splinters of hail,
One handful of dream-dust
    Not for sale.

STOKELY MALCOLM ME

i have been seeking
what i have never found
what i don't know what i want
but it must be around
i been upset
since the day before last
but that day was so long
i done forgot when it passed
yes almost forgot
what i have not found
but i know it must be
somewhere around.

you live in the Bronx
so folks say.

Stokely,
did i ever live
up your
way?
???
??
?

SLUM DREAMS

Little dreams
Of springtime
Bud in sunny air
With no roots
To nourish them,
Since no stems
Are there—
Detached,
Naïve,
So young,
On air alone
They're hung.

GEORGIA DUSK

Sometimes there's a wind in the Georgia dusk
That cries and cries and cries
In lonely pity through the Georgia dusk
Veiling what the darkness hides.

Sometimes there's blood in the Georgia dusk
Left by a streak of sun,
A crimson trickle in the Georgia dusk.
Whose blood? . . . Everyone's.

Sometimes a wind in the Georgia dusk
Scatters hate like seed
To sprout their bitter barriers
Where the sunsets bleed.

WHERE? WHEN? WHICH?

When the cold comes
With a bitter fragrance
Like rusty iron and mint,
And the wind blows
Sharp as integration
With an edge like apartheid,
And it is winter,
And the cousins of the too-thin suits
Ride on bitless horses
Tethered by something worse than pride,
Which areaway, or bar,
Or station waiting room
Will not say,
Horse and horseman, outside!
With old and not too gentle
Apartheid?

VARI-COLORED SONG

If I had a heart of gold,
As have some folks I know,
I'd up and sell my heart of gold
And head North with the dough.

But I don't have a heart of gold.
My heart's not even lead.
It's made of plain old Georgia clay.
That's why my heart is red.

I wonder why red clay's so red
And Georgia skies so blue.
I wonder why it's yes to me,
But yes, *sir*, sir, to you.

I wonder why the sky's so blue
And why the clay's so red.
Why down South is always *down,*
And never *up* instead.

JIM CROW CAR

Get out the lunch-box of your dreams
And bite into the sandwich of your heart,
And ride the Jim Crow car until it screams
And, like an atom bomb, bursts apart.

WARNING

Negroes,
Sweet and docile,
Meek, humble, and kind:
Beware the day
They change their mind!

Wind
In the cotton fields,
Gentle breeze:
Beware the hour
It uproots trees!

DAYBREAK IN ALABAMA

When I get to be a composer
I'm gonna write me some music about
Daybreak in Alabama
And I'm gonna put the purtiest songs in it
Rising out of the ground like a swamp mist
And falling out of heaven like soft dew.
I'm gonna put some tall tall trees in it
And the scent of pine needles
And the smell of red clay after rain
And long red necks
And poppy colored faces
And big brown arms
And the field daisy eyes
Of black and white black white black people
And I'm gonna put white hands
And black hands and brown and yellow hands
And red clay earth hands in it
Touching everybody with kind fingers
And touching each other natural as dew
In that dawn of music when I
Get to be a composer
And write about daybreak
In Alabama.

ABOUT THE AUTHOR

Langston Hughes was born in Joplin, Missouri, in 1902. After graduation from high school, he spent a year in Mexico with his father, then a year studying at Columbia University. His first poem in a nationally known magazine was "The Negro Speaks of Rivers," which appeared in *Crisis* in 1921. In 1925, he was awarded the First Prize for Poetry of the magazine *Opportunity*, the winning poem being "The Weary Blues," which gave its title to his first book of poems, published in 1926. As a result of his poetry, Mr. Hughes received a scholarship at Lincoln University in Pennsylvania, where he won his B.A. in 1929. In 1943, he was awarded an honorary Litt.D. by his alma mater; he has also been awarded a Guggenheim Fellowship (1935), a Rosenwald Fellowship (1940), and an American Academy of Arts and Letters Grant (1947). From 1926 until his death in 1967, Langston Hughes devoted his time to writing and lecturing. He wrote poetry, short stories, autobiography, song lyrics, essays, humor, and plays. A cross section of his work was published in 1958 as *The Langston Hughes Reader*.

THE INK DARK MOON
Love Poems by Ono no Komachi and Izumi Shikibu
Translated by Jane Hirshfield with Mariko Aratani

At once frankly erotic and profoundly spiritual, these exquisitely translated poems were written by two ladies of the Heian court of Japan between the ninth and eleventh centuries A.D.

"Sheer pleasure...Textual and cultural clutter drop away, revealing timeless, haunting images."

—Edwin A. Cranston, Harvard University

0-679-72958-5/$9.95

SELECTED POEMS
by Langston Hughes

A classic collection by the lyric voice of the Harlem Renaissance, whose poetry launched a revolution among black writers in America and celebrated the experience of men and women who had previously been invisible, in language that merges the spoken with the sung.

0-679-72818-X/$10.00

THE TALE OF GENJI
by Murasaki Shikibu
Translated and Abridged by Edward G. Seidensticker

"Not only the world's first real novel, but one of its greatest"(Donald Keene, Columbia University), *The Tale of Genji* is a lively and astonishingly nuanced portrait of a refined society where every dalliance is an act of political consequence.

0-679-72953-4/$10.00

DEMOCRACY IN AMERICA: VOLUMES I & II
by Alexis de Tocqueville
Translated by Phillips Bradley
Introduction by Daniel J. Boorstin

An enduring study of a democracy in its infancy that embraces America's history, geography, politics, legal system, economy, and culture, *Democracy in America* remains, 150 years after its completion, the most objective, thorough, and insightful work of its kind.

Vol. I: 0-679-72825-2/$9.00, Vol II: 0-679-72826-0/$8.95

____ **A Lost Lady** by Willa Cather $9.00   0-679-72887-2

____ **Death Comes for the Archbishop** by Willa Cather $9.00   0-679-72889-9

____ **My Mortal Enemy** by Willa Cather $8.95   0-679-73179-2

____ **One of Ours** by Willa Cather $12.00   0-679-73744-8

____ **The Professor's House** by Willa Cather $10.00   0-679-73180-6

____ **Forty Stories** by Anton Chekhov, $11.00   0-679-73375-2
     translated by Robert Payne

____ **A Tale of Two Cities** by Charles Dickens, $7.95   0-679-72965-8
     with an introduction by Simon Schama

____ **The Brothers Karamazov** by Fyodor Dostoevsky, $16.00   0-679-72925-9
     translated by Richard Pevear and
     Larissa Volokhonsky

____ **The Aeneid**, translated by Robert Fitzgerald $7.95   0-679-72952-6

____ **The Odyssey**, translated by Robert Fitzgerald $7.95   0-679-72813-9

____ **Madame Bovary** by Gustave Flaubert, $10.00   0-679-73636-0
     translated by Francis Steegmuller

____ **Three Classic African-American Novels**, $12.95   0-679-72742-6
     edited and with an introduction by
     Henry Louis Gates, Jr.
     Clotel by William Wells Brown,
     Iola Leroy by Frances E.W. Harper,
     The Marrow of Tradition by Charles W. Chestnutt

____ **The Sorrows of Young Werther** $8.95   0-679-72951-8
     by Johann Wolfgang von Goethe
     translated by Elizabeth Mayer and Louise Bogan,
     with a foreword by W. H. Auden

____ **The Ink Dark Moon: Love Poems** $9.95   0-679-72958-5
     by Ono No Komachi and Izumi Shikibu,
     Women of the Ancient Court of Japan,
     translated by Jane Hirshfield with Mariko Aratani

____ **The Panther and the Lash** by Langston Hughes $10.00   0-679-73659-X

___ **Selected Poems of Langston Hughes** $10.00   0-679-72818-X
     by Langston Hughes

___ **The Ways of White Folks** by Langston Hughes $9.00   0-679-72817-1

___ **Stories** by Katherine Mansfield, $11.00   0-679-73374-4
     with an introduction by Jeffrey Meyers

___ **The Republic of Plato**, translated by B. Jowett $9.00   0-679-73387-6

___ **Cyrano de Bergerac** by Edmond Rostand, $9.95   0-679-73413-9
     translated by Anthony Burgess

___ **The Tale of Genji** by Murasaki Shikibu, $10.00   0-679-72953-4
     translated and abridged by Edward Seidensticker

___ **Dr. Jekyll and Mr. Hyde** by Robert Louis Stevenson, $7.00   0-679-73476-7
     with an introduction by Joyce Carol Oates

___ **Democracy in America: Volume I** $9.00   0-679-72825-2
     by Alexis de Tocqueville,
     translated by Phillips Bradley,
     with an introduction by Daniel J. Boorstin

___ **Democracy in America: Volume II** $8.95   0-679-72826-0
     by Alexis de Tocqueville,
     translated by Phillips Bradley

Available at your bookstore or call toll-free to order: 1-800-733-3000.
Credit cards only. Prices subject to change.